To:

From:

Date:

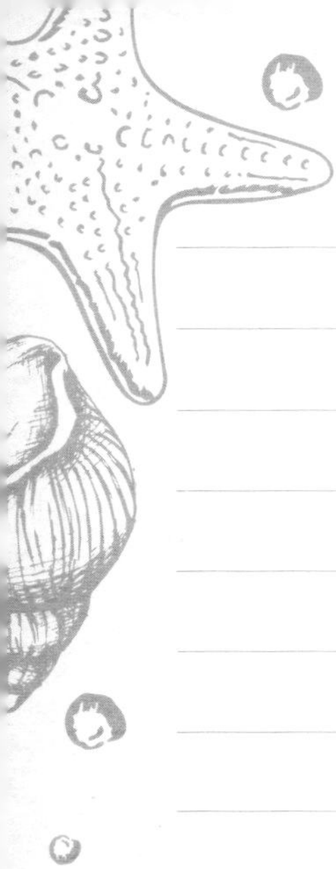

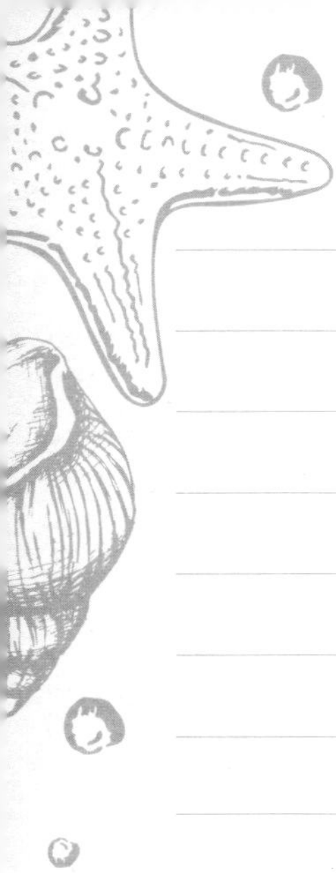

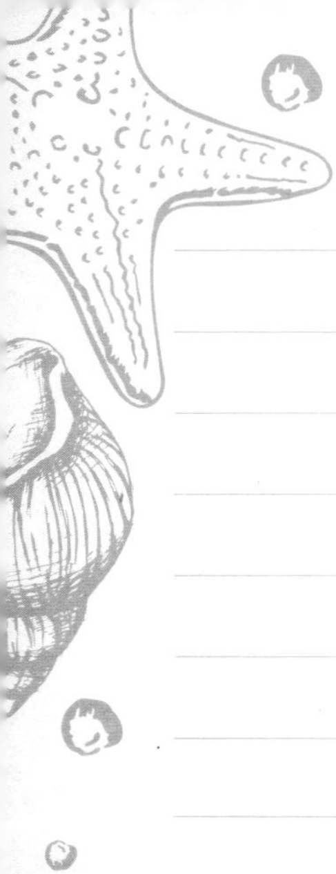

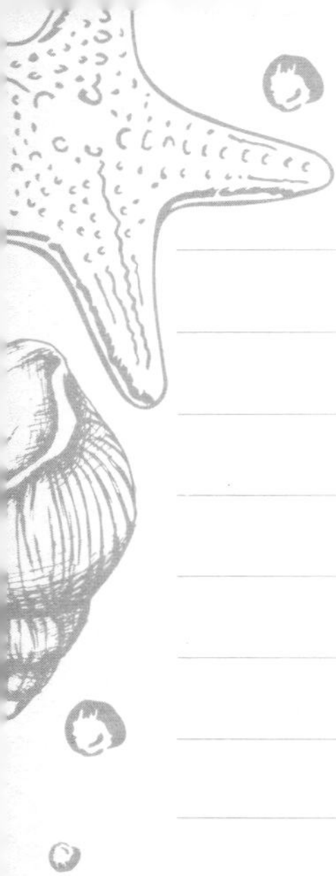

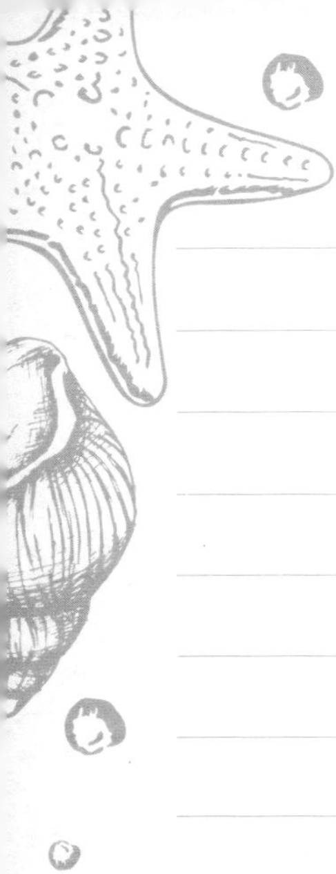

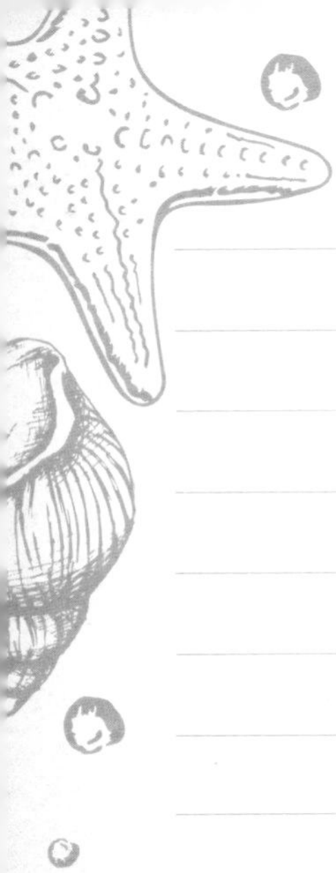

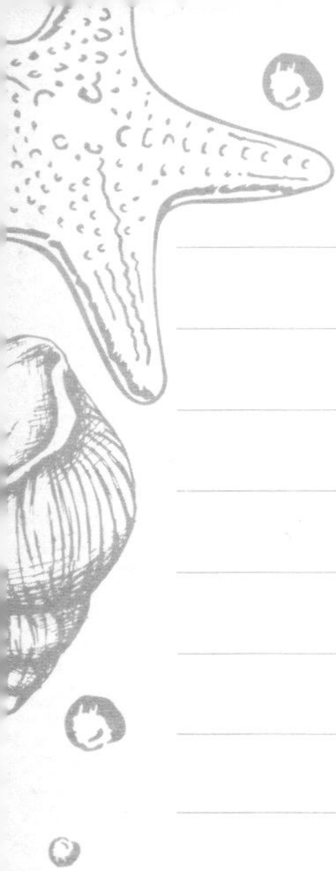

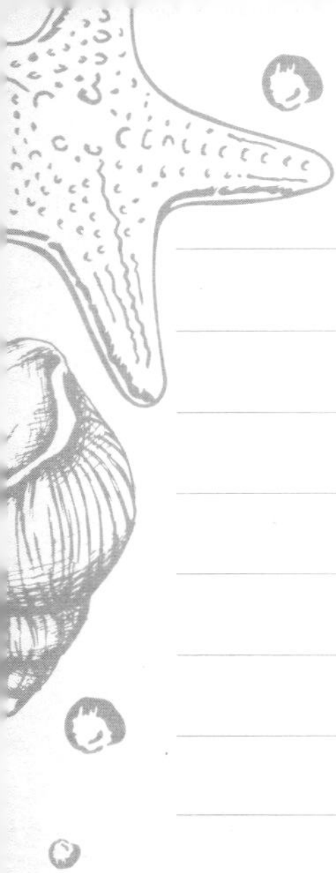

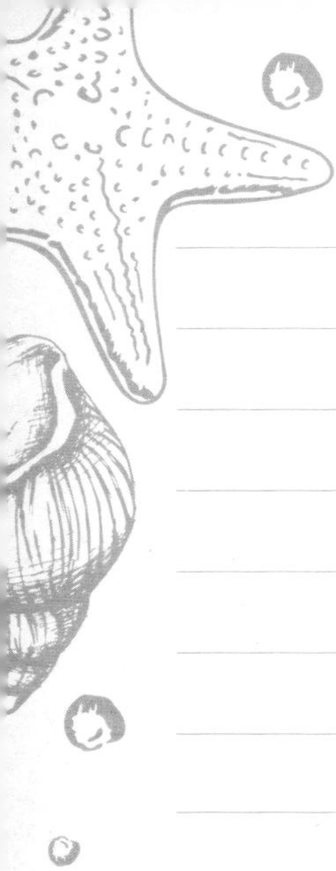

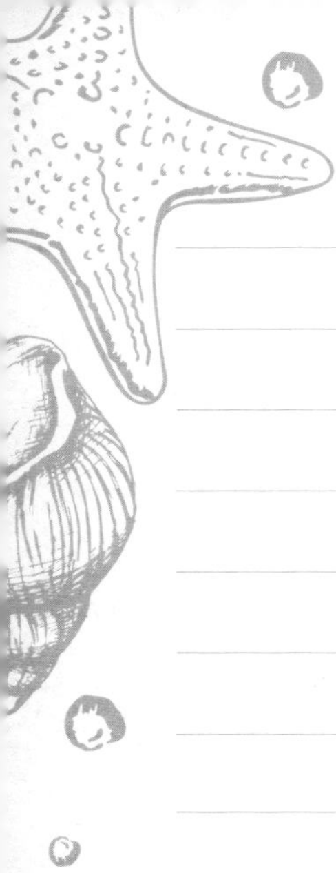

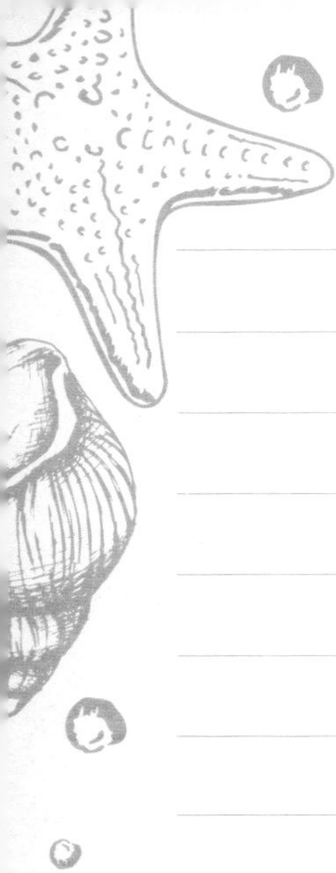

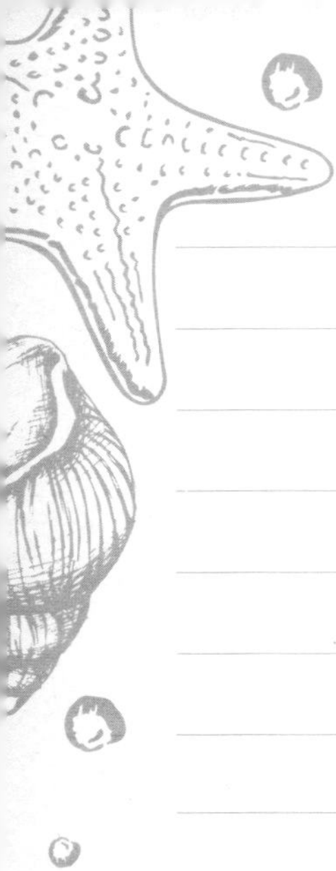

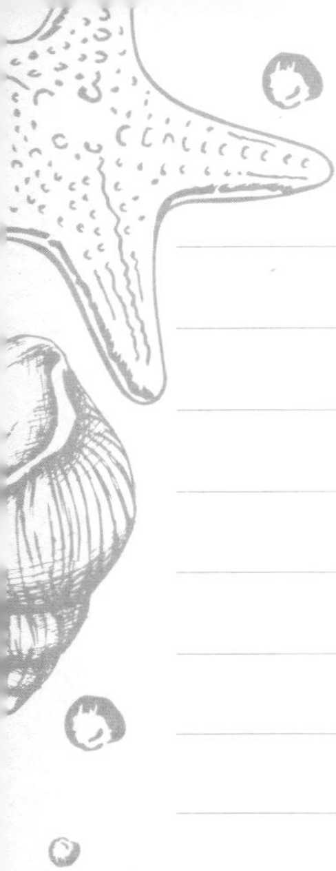

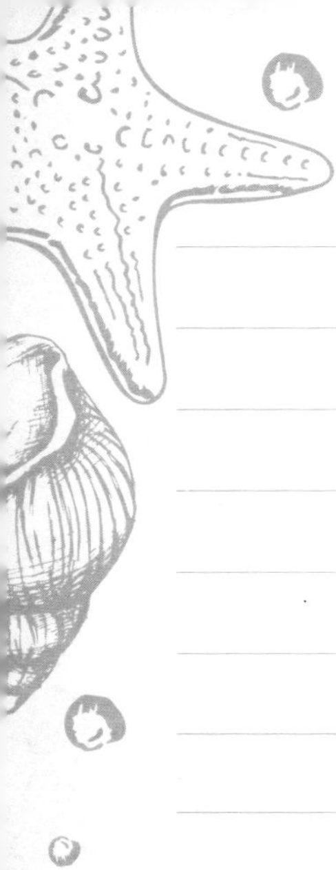

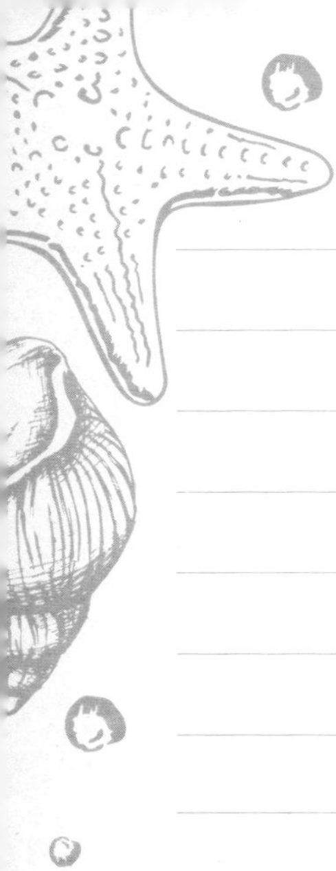

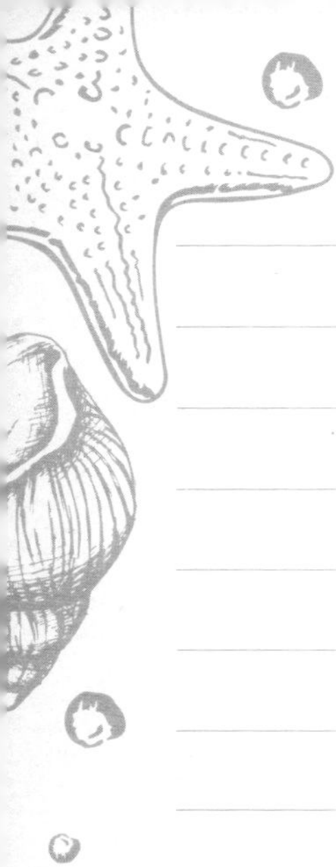

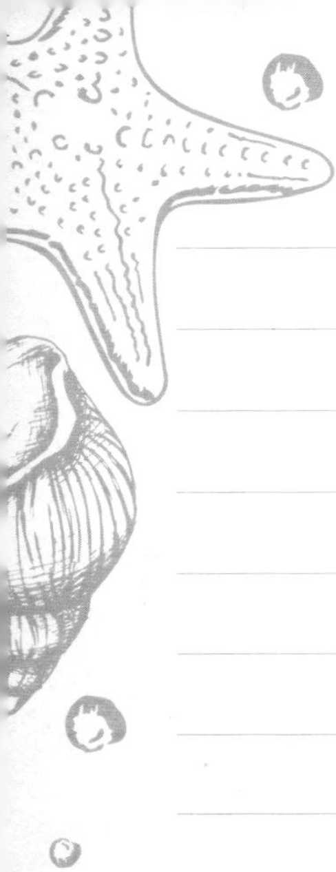

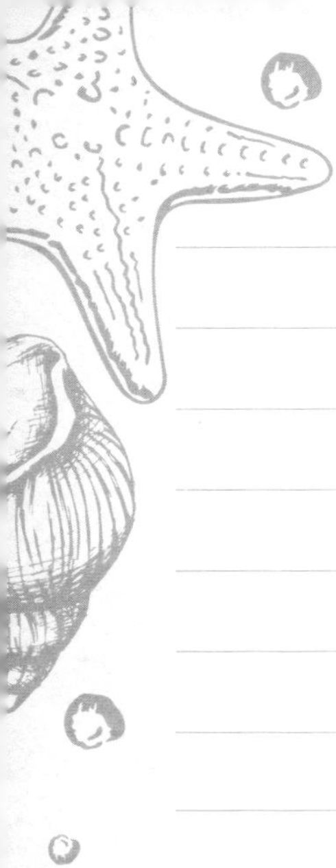

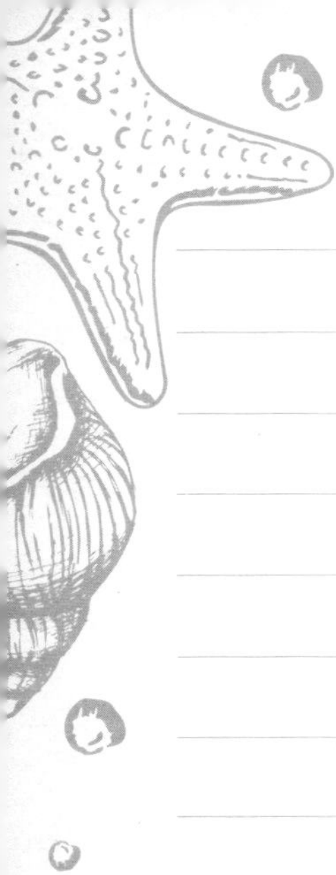

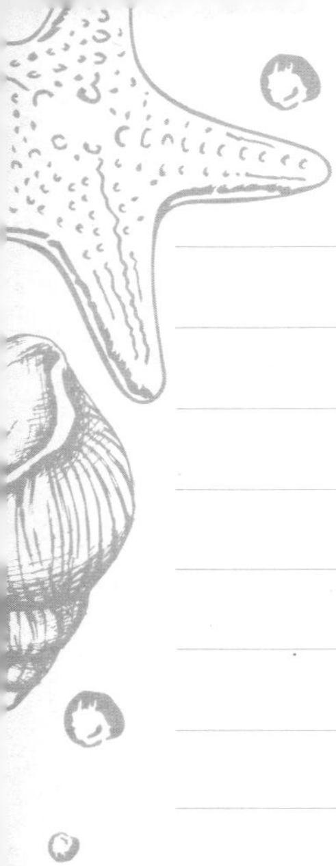

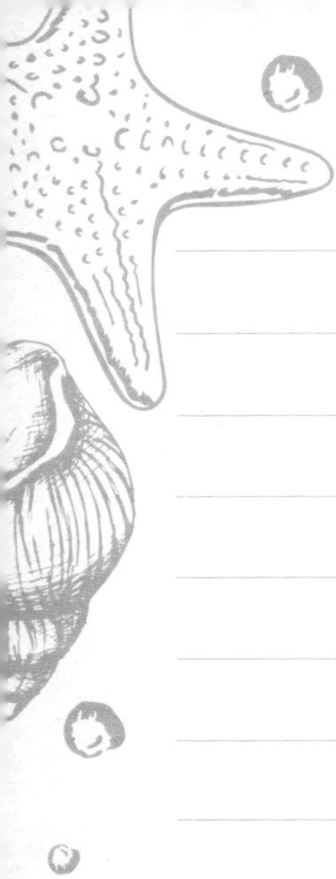

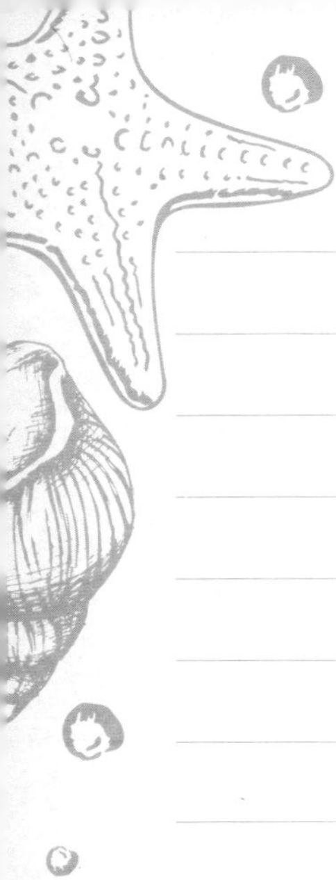

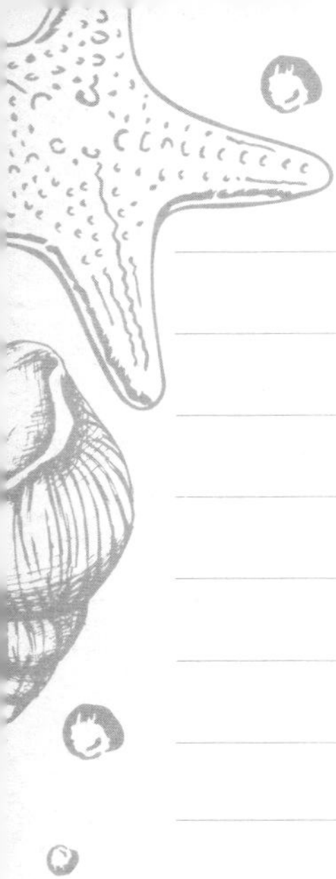

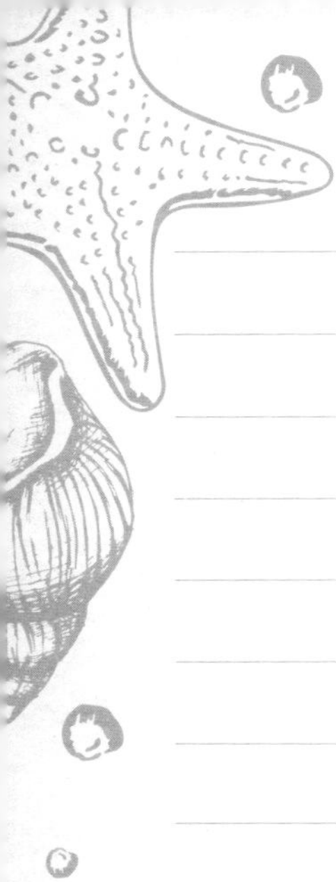

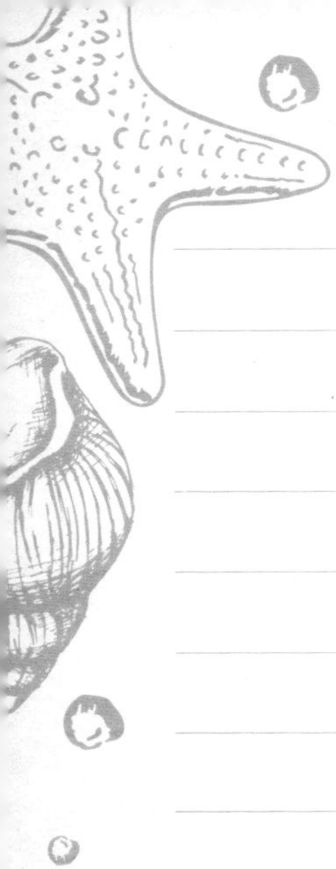

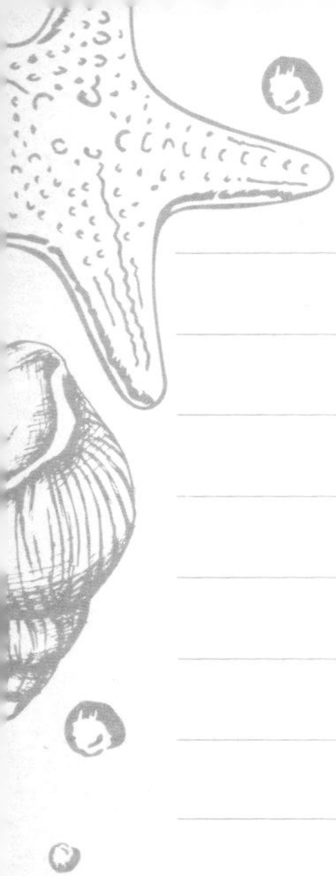